The Color of a Woman's Heart

Her Soul has borrowed flesh and bone from her mother earth, to walk amongst us. For she is more than the eye and mind can conceive. This Spirit of Light we call Woman.
~~ Casey ~~

Copyright © 2010 Casey S. Leasure
Second Printing Revised 2011
ISBN: 978-0-615-43450-6
Printed in the United States of America
Library of Congress Registration TX 7-434-441

Other books by author Casey S. Leasure
The Awakened Woman
ISBN # 9781628907032

Oneness of Soul
ISBN # 9780615576633

The Color of a Woman's Heart
Is published in the Italian language by:
Auralia Edizioni, Italy, www.auralia-edizioni.com,
Il Colore del Cuore di Una Donna
ISBN: 9788897008095

THIS BOOK IS PUBLISHED
BY
CASEY S. LEASURE

All rights reserved ®. No part of this book may be used or reproduced by any mean, graphic, electronic, or mechanical, including photocopy, recording, taping or by any information storage retrieval system without the written permission of the author, except in the case of brief quotations embodied in critical articles and reviews.

~ Thank You ~

Let these be the spoken words of the consciousness of oneness. The whispers in the distance wind you long to hear. The wings that embrace you and carry you to the mountain tops and across the oceans to your deepest truths. Hold my hand as I dance with the thoughts and hearts of who you are. Let my words drip upon you like honey from the kingdom of heaven as you read the poems written on my wings before you awaken from your dreams.

This Book is dedicated to:

All the women of the world and the true nature of their being.
Much love to each and every one of you.
~ Casey ~

Contents

	Page
The Color of a Woman's Heart	*1*
Angel Woman	*144*
Moon Woman	*160*
Butterfly Woman	*173*
The Gospel of Woman	*189*
Lovers	*193*
Dancing with Life	*211*
Woman and Horse	*213*
Woman and the Angel	*214*
To Dance Upon a Rainbow	*215*
The Child at the Pond	*217*
Her Song	*219*

1

Beautiful is the woman who is in flight of her freedom.
Soaring to heights above all she had ever thought before.
She touches the sun and laughs, dancing across the sky.
Unstoppable in her dreams now, she is the Phoenix.

She closes her eyes and raises her hands to touch the source of all creations as her heart sings for the love of life.
In solitude but far from alone she meets with her angels as they greet her with respect and love.
The power of her magic is not in spells, nor is it in her sacred dance.
Her power is drawn upon the color of her heart.

A woman can hear the song of a flower as it blossoms with life. She hears the beauty in the voice of the night that whispers so softly to her as the stars sing to her.
The angels come to watch her in all her beauty as she touches life with her gentle eyes and healing thoughts that caress the weak and forgotten creatures that walk our earth.
Woman sees all life with the colors of her heart.

4

Butterflies dance around the fragrance of her inner beauty as they wish only to sip the nectar of her song.
She has freed herself of the bondage of lies that trapped her, as she steps into a new world of love for her truth and knowledge of the woman she is. Dancing on her journey she now sees all life through the color of a woman's heart.

Embrace the Consciousness of Oneness, let your Spirit dance, be the vibration of Love that you are.
Listen to the song of your heart that beats to the rhythm of your Soul.
Hear the Spirit of God calling you, and rejoice in the connection of your AWAKENING.

I say young girl, hear my words!
Dream of castles and knights in shining armor,
dream of hero's coming to your rescue.
Dream of beautiful homes with white picket fences.
Dream of love and romance if you so desire.
But let no man dictate your dreams nor take
ownership of your heart.
To share your dreams and maintain your dignity of
self is the color of a woman's heart.

Bathed in the Light of her being, woman rests with her thoughts of love, life, and peace.
She paints her thoughts as though she is spending all her time in the company of angels, surrounded by music so beautiful and peaceful that even wild beasts become quiet to listen.
Her thoughts of love draw the stars of the galaxy closer to her, to see the colors of a woman's heart.

She smiles in contemplation of serving her God. Resting her head upon her altar in the garden she waits. Knowing her God will never turn eyes away from her.
She sacrifices all earthly desires to be with her God.

*All around the world Women of the Light will walk hand in hand with the giants, they will sleep beneath the stars with these beasts in peace.
They will sing lullabies to the dancing warriors who cry for war and subdue them to a state of brotherly love for each other.
These Women of the Light do not adhere to the lies of fear and hate because they live through the Source of Love.*

She listens to the voice of her soul, she hears the song of all life.
Quiet in her world at times, she just breathes life.
She thinks in color as she listens to the thoughts in her mind.
Above all else she is true to herself and her highest good as she holds hands with love and dances with the angels.
The beautiful music she hears is in the color of her heart.

Behold,
You are the light that was sent to do the work.
You are the human angel through the creative energy of thought. In your heart, your mind, your soul, you hold the records to all that we are.
Your path is necessary, so stay the course.

Surrounded by the music in the light woman embraces the echoes of her soul.
Her journey is one of compassion and kindness to all creation as she is connected to the Great Consciousness of Oneness.
Her desire to live in peace with all life shows everyone the color of a woman's heart.

13

Woman will hear the whispers of her song coming from the mountain tops, as she dances in the dream time of her dawn.
She will awaken to Angels gathering around her to bathe her with love and dress her in a garment of sun light and flowers for they know she is on a path of new beginnings.

The Gods adore the beauty of her heart as she dances before them.
The Angels they circle around her swaying in rhythm as her heart sings to them.
Giants chase leafs on the ground laughing and yelling as she moves the wind through her vibration of love.
This they say is the color of a woman's heart.

Climb upon this gentle giants back woman in that time between dream worlds of your realities.
Let his spirit carry yours, in a fast gallop through the sky, leaping over rainbow racing past the Sun cheering you on.
Ride this sprit to the heavens of dancing flowers and singing trees in open meadows of laughter.
Where the breeze in your face is the brush of angel wings gliding alongside you.
Go woman, and ride side by side with chariots of joy, peace, and happiness.
Look around woman, your riding in the heart of the great consciousness of your God, the all loving creative energy of your every wish and desire.

The song of your soul is in rhythm with the thoughts of your heart, which is the dance of your journey.
Let your consciousness of love surround you in the words you breathe, as you sing your song and dance your story.
Wear your oneness of life so all will see your highest good.
As you show them the color of a woman's heart.

In her thoughts she will embrace the many colors of her love.
She will paint a poem across the sky for all to see.
She will write a prayer across the water for all to bathe in. Her heart is one with the Consciousness of her God.
Woman smiles at the Angels as she creates love in the world.

*What beautiful thoughts she has about her journey
of life as she grows closer to the truth of who she is.
It is in the still waters of her my mind she floats so
freely with the images of her higher self.
Her choice is to live in harmony with the angels and
the elements that touch her so gently with love.
Woman sows the garden of her mind with the color
of her heart as she plants her love and abundance
to grow.*

In love with the words of her soul woman dances to the song in her heart.
As though her thoughts were her partner she moves to the rhythm of the music she hears.
In love with the Spirit, her dance is one of a new day.

When a woman meditates she will touch the consciousness of her God.
She will walk through the halls of her mind pouring bottles of liquid golden light over her thoughts as she clears her head.
Woman stands in the silence of the universe with the creative source of love as the light paints the color of her heart.

*The soul of woman is the Heart of God.
Her spirit dance is that of Mother Earth.
She embraces all life from the smallest flower
to the giant creatures that walk the world.
Woman is and always will be the symbol of
Joy, Peace, and Compassion in her independence.*

*Woman is the music of the wind.
She is the dance of Angels in flight.
Her Spirit is the song of the stars in the sky and she touches the heart of the beast with her whispers of love.
She weaves the fabric of her world with love, kindness, joy and peace, as she lives to create a pool of thoughts that dance around her. Like spirits in the colors of her heart.*

The vibration of love is a life within itself that bends around the whole experience of our being, as it touches lives all around the world far and near.
Say a name in love and it will reach them no matter where they are.
Paint a color with love and it will spread across the sky.
Express a feeling of love and the whole world will feel it.

Woman lays herself across the altar of her mind, in her Holiest of Holy thoughts.
She lives in the heart of her God.
Her relationship with love is adored even by the Angels as they shelter her with their wings.
Her compassion and kindness feeds the hungry that are scared and lonely as she anoints all life with the color of a woman's heart.

In your soul you are manifested in perfect balance of being.
You are the creation of absolute knowledge and Love.
A unique dance, a beautiful song, and a magnificent story to tell.
Yes, yes this is who you really are!
This is what is unfolding. Dance your life, sing with others, tell your story, it's perfect!

Woman stands before the Gods undaunted by their clamoring and growls.
She claims before them the True Law is not in a book nor is it written by man.
She softly explains that the words are written across her heart, across her eyes and all over the skin and throughout her body.
They have been recorded by her soul, the first thoughts ever spoken aloud.
The skies grow silent, as a single light shines through cascading over her.

Woman will hold the beauty of her consciousness in one hand, and the journey of her soul in the other. As she will bring these old companions together in her song to the heavens, the angels will dance with delight and the creatures of the earth will welcome her path.
For she will be known by the colors of her heart.

As if she were riding on the tail of a star gliding across the galaxy, woman feels the breath of God touching her.
She knows her soul and hears the words as though it were angels lifting her up to the heavens.
With her understanding of this journey she just simply and gracefully moves in to the next level of her purpose with the color of a woman's heart.

Let the songs and the poems of the Angels flow through your mind as they dance with your thoughts.
Let us touch the color of our voice as we speak to each other with kindness and love.
Raise your eyes to the heavens of a stranger as you pass them on the street.
Hold my hands as I lift you to your highest truth and we will rise like smoke in the air and into the heart of God.

Beautiful are the flowers of the meadow, as you watch the branches softly sway back and forth in the wind.
You can see the spirits touching her hair as they kiss her face. The grass, it cushions her feet that touch the ground.
Is that the melody of the angels I hear?
Maybe it's all just an illusion.
Maybe all I really see is the color of a woman's heart.

*She lives in the thoughts of benevolence for all life.
In her solitude she calls forth the kingdom of love
and light.
As she walks through life with the Oneness of
Consciousness of all things.
Behold the messenger within her, a single dove of
love.*

Freed from her hurt and sorrow, no longer tainted by past relationships she embraces her spirit. Unstoppable in her endeavors to live her life she makes only one commitment "to be true to the colors of her heart".

Quietly the forest watches her scared dance as she moves in oneness with her soul.
Her thoughts are in rhythm with the movement of her dance as she invokes the angels of love and compassion to touch all life, to heal all people.

Freed from torturous thoughts, woman meditates on a majestic space.
It is the landscape of her inner world full of serenity and peace.
Like the wolf that runs off into the forest after being wounded by the hunter and lies down to meditate and heals.
Women creates this world in her mind and heals, as she lays her thoughts to rest in the colors of her heart.

The Awakened Woman delights in her path of Self Realization.
Like a meadow of flowers welcomes the rain to help them grow.
Woman welcomes the Consciousness of Love as her food for Truth.
Her path to Love and Truth is the same path as the stars are to the Heavens.

Her pain is but only an eclipse from the truth.
She knows the lies are the darkness trying to cast
fear into her.
Focusing on the higher truth for love, she continues
to journey the path to find her treasure buried deep
within her heart.
In her perseverance the eclipse passes and the light
returns to shine again on the color of a woman's
heart.

The song of a butterfly's heart is heard as clear and loud as that of a giant's heart, when it is sung to the Spirit of Creation.
Just as the Spirit of Creation see the dance of a crippled man is just as beautiful as the dance of a ballerina when he dances to the beat of the song in his heart.

How beautiful a spirit you are, surrounded by the vibration of your soul.
Greeting life with a loving kindness, and compassion, you are one with the Universe.
As your thoughts of creativity dance in your mind, you show others a path of love.

They see her in their consciousness of oneness as her soul reflects upon all life.
So beautiful is her heart for all creation.
So loving is her presence.
Her true power lies in how she carries herself through her endeavors.
Her soul lights the way for other mortals who are weakened on their Journey.

In her solitude she meditates on the beauty of her world.
It is there she becomes centered on who she really is, and finds the knowledge of her higher purpose.
This is her chosen path to share with all life.
As she knows her wisdom comes from her direct link to the source of all creation.

She touches the hearts of those she dances around, as though her magical thoughts could make fallen petals reattach themselves to the flower.
She will call upon the song of the Sun with the voice of her soul and create images of hearts in the clouds with the movement of her hands.
Her love for life will look like the palette of an artist painting a master piece as her canvas will look like the color of a woman's heart.

In the center of her universe, woman stands with beauty beyond words. Guided by her soul, she journeys down the road of compassion for all life. Her thoughts are like magic with the power to create a path in her world that draws from the Oneness with all that is.

What a beautiful experience it is for you to hear the voice of your soul.
This voice of eternity, who has journeyed so far through time. The voice that lives in all of us. That speaks of a path of loving kindness and compassion for all life. Your oneness of being.

Let the beauty of your soul radiate about you.
Share the words of your heart all around you.
Make your thought about the love within you.
You are such a unique individual.
In this oneness of life all around you.

Be the song of your Heart, the words of your Soul, and dance in the Light of Creation.
Be the Consciousness of Love, the Consciousness of Oneness, seeing and touching all life for its Highest Good.

She dances to the sound of the ocean, her partner is the wind. The sky and the sun watch in joy as she dances and laughs.
Each breath is a new beginning for her to love more.
Sharing her joy and love with all life is the color of a woman's heart.

She is like a stream flowing softly through her thoughts.
Gently touching her memories, listening to the melody of her desires, woman aligns herself with the universe of abundance.
Embracing her opportunities as keys to the doors she seeks to open.

She plays her favorite song, tells her favorite joke, and giggles to herself about the things she has heard.
Oh how she loves to feel good about her inner world and the company she keeps within.
As she dresses her joy in pretty colors and dances with her thoughts of love.
Laughing at the way she laughs, woman holds hands with creatures of pleasure as she walks through her day, because she is, the color of her heart.

Hold your hand to the sky that we may touch once more.
Breathe deeply so that our spirits may merge.
Touch the water in the stream with your hand so I can feel your love as I drink.
Send your thoughts to the stars that I may hear the music at night, and dance to the color of a woman's heart.

So magical are her thoughts, and so beautiful is her love for life. The woman finds her freedom in the power of her thinking, as she creates her world of balance and harmony through her thoughts of the Oneness with the Universe.
This they say is the color of a woman's heart.

Woman's love vibrates in color, because her life is full of color. This vibration extends throughout the galaxies.
When her love encompasses you it does not divide and separate. The vibration gently bends around the whole experience.
This is how her oneness of love moves.

So delicate was her color, as she walked with The Christ.
His words gracing her life as she listened and walked by His side. Present in heart and mind she loved Him and He loved her.
This woman Mary Magdalene and the color of her heart.
For I too know the love He has for the color of a woman's heart.

*A woman who sits in quiet contemplation of her heart and her soul is in good company.
Making your thoughts of a more gentle love.
Close your eyes and draw in your most beautiful thoughts and embrace them and love them and welcome them.
Listen to the Oneness of your consciousness.
Can you see the colors of your heart?
They dance before you, entering your mind, filling you with joy for Life and Love.*

To look into the reflection of your eyes is to greet your angel face on.
Comprised of all light and all energy your path is one that moves to the music in your mind, the words of your soul, and the beat of your heart.
She will bathe herself in the love of her God, as she journeys through life showing everyone the color of a woman's heart.

At times woman will step off the path to find out why she must stay on the path.
The storms will no longer dominate her message nor her journey.
Woman will rise above the storm as she dances in the rain back on to her path of Self Realization moving closer to her higher truth and her purpose in life.

Woman's thoughts will flow as deeply as that of natures.
In her solitude she will touch the love in her mind.
As if she were one with the elements of life, a tree at the pond, or a butterfly with a flower.
Her journey is pure beauty with her God.
As she lets go and follows the colors of her heart.

Created in the Consciousness of her God, Woman is and always will be the breathing heart of this all loving energy force.
Spirit cannot be broken, it cannot be corralled. Woman will race the wind, dance in the Sun and live the joy of Spirit, for she is and always will be the breathing heart of her God.

A woman can hear the song of a flower as it blossoms with life.
She hears the beauty in the voice of the night that whispers so softly to her, as the stars sing to her.
The angels come to watch her, in all her beauty as she touches life with her gentle eyes and healing thoughts that caress the weak and forgotten creatures that walk our earth.
Woman sees all life with the colors of her heart.

Deep within a woman's soul is a light that shines so brightly that if you could see it with the human eye it would blind you.
Yet it is the oneness of all life the loving creativity energy of all things.
It brings everything together and is the source that helps us to heal one another.
It is the light woman uses to create the world around her.

Woman is comprised of all light and all energy her path is one that moves to the music in her mind, the words of her soul, and the beat of her heart.
She will bathe herself in the love of her God, as she journeys through life showing everyone the color of a woman's heart.

How sweet the sound of her soul is that speaks as a whole to all the people.
Like a voice that echo's throughout the universe and in every cell of her body, she will share her song.
Her soul so bold and beautiful stands untainted by the clamoring voices that would unsuccessfully try to weaken the truth of who she is.

Woman's Spirit will stand as one from the sea to the highest mountain her words will be heard as though it was the winds of the sky and written in the clouds we see.
Her truth is the voice of her soul that touches the skin of our earth as she dances with the breathing heart of her God that cascades her every step.

*Woman will quietly look into the forest of her mind.
She will breathe the air of Spirit into her thoughts.
Looking into the reflection of her dreams woman
will cast her desires before her God.*
*Above all else woman's desire will seek to know her
highest good in life and know her path is one with
all creation.*
*It will be in this oneness of life that she will find her
serenity and peace, for in this oneness she will find
the colors of her heart.*

*In a woman's mind she creates a sacred dance.
She dances in the world between the heavens
and the earth.
As her dance weaves a garment of oneness around
the worlds, she will whisper the words of
compassion and kindness into the ears of all people.
They will feel her dance upon their skin as she leads
them into the new world of one love for all creation.*

Woman puts her ear to the wind and listens the words "you are so worthy"
Woman turns her face to the sun and closes her eyes to see the angels of joy reach down to kiss her and pull her up.
She will bend her thoughts like a rainbow as she dances with her creative energies.
She will touch the colors of all sounds the universe sends her way. Behold her song!
It is the color of a Woman's heart.

Far above our universe,
Beyond our very galaxies
The color of a woman's heart,
Is created in the Consciousness of her God.

The angels sing to her as if they were the wind moving through her.
The heavens open up as if to reach down and lay a path of roses and butterflies before her.
Woman touches the lives of all creation as she dances and sings of the love she offers to share through the colors of her heart.

In the consciousness of God plays the melody of woman.
She is the music the stars dance to, she is the bend in the rainbow.
Woman is the glorious sound of the wind blowing across the ocean.
She is the seamless garment of colors that dress the earth we walk upon.
Woman is the whisper that calms the raging beast that blindly charges at the darkness of the night.
She is the voice heard in the dreamers' mind of love and romance.
Woman is and always will be the breathing heart of God.

Designed as an interrogate part of the universe.
Woman will see herself through the eyes of
The Loving Creative Energy of Consciousness
As her Soul speaks woman listens to the colors
of her heart.

In the Soul of every woman is the record of her creation between an all loving creative force in heaven and her Mother Earth from whose womb, woman was birthed.
For every woman is the High Priestess who carries the teachings of compassion, kindness, and love for all creation.
As she dances the colors of her heart the children will follow.

Woman rests at the center of her God's heart, she dreams of beautiful dances and sweet candy made of nectar.
She is the waking thought of the sunrise, the scent of morning dew.
All flowers want to grow up to be a woman.

It was on the canvas of life that her soul was the paint brush her God used to create such a master piece.
Her consciousness would be the pen in which her journey would be written for the many lives she would live.
The angels would stand in choir and sing as such a glorious creation was prepared.
As the stars in heavens are the true record keepers of the Creation of Woman.

In the Kingdom of Heaven the music of a woman's spirit is played, it is heard in the winds across the earth and is the song of the stars in our galaxy. The majestic dance of woman can be seen in the clouds reflecting on a lake.

Her Spirit is one with the gentle giants that race through the forest and the meadows, wild and free. As her thoughts of life and love are dressed in the consciousness of oneness her beauty is seen through the color of a woman's heart.

Joy is the laughter of a woman reflecting the beauty of our universe.
Holy is the sound the word "woman" makes when it is spoken. Woman bares her heart in the mists of adversity and calamity, bringing light onto despair. Woman holds hands with the angels singing and dances before the world as she transform into Spirit of light.

Often while a woman sleeps the angels of heaven and earth will gather around her and sing glorious songs of her journey and recite poems of her beauty.
As they anoint her body with holy colors and vibrations of the consciousness of her God.
This they say fills the color of her heart.

Let the great consciousness of oneness draw you into their thoughts of joy and pleasure, listen to the music of the universe and feel it pull you into the sacred dance of love.
Let your body rise to this majestic creative energy of all life, and let it fill you with the voice that colors your heart designed for your journey.

So beautiful is the dream world of the sleeping.
In a time that spirits dance in meadows of poppies
The willows dance to the music of rainbows and sun shine.
When she will see the color of sound and fly with the angels to the mountain tops.

She will listening to the elements sing in harmony and watches the clouds as they change colors and formations.
It is there she dances in the silence, with the lover who sees the color of her heart.

No longer corralled nor tethered by the opinions of others, woman becomes like the wild mustang on the plains as her spirit races across the skies, leading the pack, jumping sun rays and following the music in her soul.
She leans her thoughts towards her castle where her freedom reins.

Woman will dance upon the rainbows in all her glory.
She will shout out to the world from the mountain tops.
Woman knows Her Oneness, Her Truth, and Her Path ….
As the eagle soars above the clouds her spirit rides the wind of love.

She smiles in contemplation of her all loving God.
Resting upon her altar in the garden of her mind,
she waits.
Knowing her God will never turn eyes away from
her.
Her only desire is to be One with the Consciousness
of her God.

In the echoes of her mind she hears the calling "woman create."
Woman answers the calling as she touches the voice of her soul.
As though she were a wolf running through the forest in the night, she will create a dance that awakens all life around her, one of freedom and love for all creation.

We will touch the colors of our silence with our hearts.
As we create a fabric made of love, kindness, and joy that we will wrap each other in.
Each of us will hear the music of our universe play a sweet melody that we will dance our lives to, as we hold hands with Spirit into the eternity of life.

Woman's relationship with Spirit cannot be defined by man.
She will commune with creatures through the language of her heart.
Their souls will race across the desert, swim across the oceans, they will leap over rainbows and together touch the stars.
Yet to the observer it will only look as though they are standing still. Spirit on the other hand, watched it all happen.

Woman defines her understanding of love in her dance with life. She hears the music of the universe in her Oneness of Consciousness.
Gently she moves like a butterfly across the thoughts in her mind.
Woman heals the world with her dance of kindness and compassion.

Woman feels the spirit of all creation as she centers herself in thoughts of oneness with the universe.
Her vibration will rise and soar like an eagle in the sky, as her heart will be heard all around the world, one heart in rhythm with all life.
Her thoughts will kiss the stars in the heaven as her message echoes in the ears of all life.
We are the creative loving energy that will change the world.

Woman is unwilling to live in the bondage of chattering shadows that once told her what she would be.
Her new understanding of the higher truth of which she is, rides in the forefront of all her thoughts. Woman will live her understanding of her true Womanhood as though she rode on the back of the wind with joy.

Woman journeys a path of Self Realization as she follows the voice of her soul.
Neither book nor man will dictate this map to her. The treasures of who she is will be found only by her and she will share them with the women of the world as each will discover their own.

Woman understands that the reflection of her life is a mirror for her personal growth and knowledge of the journey she is on.
She will listen to her feelings and not the discounting of what others may think of them.
Woman has learned from her past that the voice of her soul will not mislead her nor lie about what she is being shown.

Woman will hear the songs and the poems of the Angels flow through her mind as they dance with her thoughts.
She touches the colors of her words as they speak of kindness and love.
Woman raises her eyes to the heavens in love of the stranger she passes on the street.
She will hold hands with her thoughts as she is lifted to her highest truth and rises like smoke in the air into the Consciousness of her God.

Woman will take many paths as she journeys through this life.
This time she will not look back, she will have no chattering shadows of regrets to chase her this time.
She will only listen to the music of new beginnings that play before her.
Disguised as butterflies her angels escort her.
Woman softly moves forward guided by her soul, holding the hands with the present as she knows all is well.

Woman moves to the beat of an ancient song.
She dances to a rhythm that is heard by all women of the world.
It is their sacred dance for all life.
It is the dance of Oneness for all Creation.

Woman will touch her many thoughts of peace and harmony throughout today.
She will touch the voice of her soul and feel the breath upon her body.
She will touch many lives with this Love, for the Angels have come and touched her highest beauty, her truest thoughts, and her greatest compassion for all life.
Woman will hold hands with the loving heart of her God, as she holds hands with all the people of her world and bring kindness and compassion to those around her.

Woman will touch the light that she is.
She will light the path for those who fear the darkness. Woman will touch the voice that sings the song of her beauty.
She will pass the song on to all women of the world. Woman will embrace the creative loving energy of life, and she will teach this to those who have lost their dance.

Woman writes her song of the Consciousness of her God.
She will feel the texture of her poem as her pen touches the paper.
She will see the many colors of this love she holds with all her thoughts.
For she will dance her highest truth with all women of the world, that the many colors of her heart come from this Consciousness of Love.

How beautiful a spirit you are, surrounded by the vibration of your soul.
Greeting life with a loving kindness, and compassion, you are one with the Universe.
As your thoughts of creativity dance in your mind, you show others a path of love.

*What beautiful thoughts she has about her journey
of life as she grows closer to the truth of who she is.
It is in the still waters of her my mind she floats so
freely with the images of her higher self.
Her choice is to live in harmony with the angels and
the elements that touch her so gently with love.
Woman sows the garden of her mind with the color
of her heart as she plants her love and abundance
to grow.*

Carved upon each star is the story of the creation of woman.
Written across the night is the story of her journey.
Shamans gaze into the fire as the chant her ancient prayers.
Woman is seen in the morning Sun as she awakens our world.

Come, come into my mind, my soul, and listen as I whisper the ancient stories through my breath. My heart remembers you, as my soul rejoices in our dance. Come, and I will sing to you a song that heals our world.

Deep in the forest of a woman's mind she finds the light of her soul.
Embracing her path she will rise above adversity with laughter and song, for she knows the truth and truth has set her free from the chattering shadows that once nipped at her heels.
Woman stands in the light and rises above the forest.

Woman and her soul are like the tigress and her jungle.
As the tigress is in oneness, a dance with the jungle, woman is in oneness, a dance with her soul, they both feel the life force that surrounds their every breath and step.
Their journey is one heart with all creation.

*Gold is bright by day, the stars will shine at night.
As diamonds will glisten in the sun light and a
beautiful song will brighten spirits in the night.
But Woman, Awakened, is bright with splendor day
and night.*

Holy, Holy, Holy, are the thoughts of woman as she touches the heart of the rising Sun.
She is One with the Consciousness that turns the earth.
Woman writes the poem that sparks the fire that dances upon the dawn as she greets the new day.
Her healing light touches all far and near as she walks her path of peace.
Holy, Holy, Holy are the thoughts of woman as she touches the hearts of all life.

In all women there is an inner light force.
Within that light there is an intelligence of creative energy manifesting her greatest awakening, to her highest good and greatest potential of the path she will journey on.
See the light in all things, acknowledge it always, and use it to heal yourself and others, use it to help all things grow. Expose your inner light to all. It is the Light of Love.

In the echoes of her mind she hears the calling "woman create."
Woman answers the calling as she touches the voice of her soul.
As though she were a wolf running through the forest in the night, she will create a dance that awakens all life around her, one of freedom and love for all creation.

In the highest heaven, in the kingdom of God.
Is the Creative Loving Energy of Thought.
Behold ...... The Creation of Woman!

It is in her solitude that she worships her Mother Earth and Heavenly Father from which she came. Angels come to minister to her the knowledge she seeks. Whole is her soul from which the source comes.
The source of all things, all creations, for all time.

Let us touch the heart of our song as we raise our consciousness of oneness and listen to the angels sing in glory of our awakenings.
We will dance in the fields of our mind with thoughts of joy, laughter, kindness and compassion for all creation.
Let us walk in life looking through the eyes of your God, feeling and listening to the kingdom of heaven here on earth for you are and always have been the breathing heart of God.

Look upon the mountain woman, look into the valley.
Your spirituality flows like a stream from the heavens, through your mind, body and out through your healing words.
You fill the cup of the one who thirsts for truth and wisdom as they seek the path you're on.

Many times on her journey woman will meet herself face to face.
She will look into the eyes of who she is in her reflection. Sometimes she will try to avoid this encounter.
Other times she will embrace it with love and the Great Compassion. Because woman knows the Oneness of her life.

Raise your thoughts to the consciousness of your God.
It is there you hear the whispers of an eternal life. A poem of absolute beauty written just for you, a song of love held just for you and a glorious mirror of who you really are. For you are and always will be the breathing heart of your God.

Soft and gentle is the voice of the woman who journeys the path of Self Realization.
As her Spirit dances across the sky lightly touching the mountain tops and then in a dive to the ocean she rides the wind in laughter and joy.
Dressed in her awakening, woman reflects the oneness of life around the world.

The music in her soul sways her body free of all fear.
She gently dances the sacred dance of life.
Present for all creation, connected to her Spirit, she is the healer who brings peace.
With her song, she will bend softly around you, touching your life with her melody of love.

Woman is like the Angel of the Garden, cultivated by the Consciousness of Oneness.
For blessed is the fruit of her life as the fragrance of her words sing to all people of the world.
It is in her garden of wisdom that others will come to harvest her knowledge of peace and compassion on their journey through life.
Her garden of love is ever growing as we seek this Angel of the Garden we call Woman.

The silent woman breathes deep, she embraces her spirit.
Clearing her mind, she stands with empty thoughts.
As wisdom comes to fill her with compassion for her journey.
She will drink truth from her thoughts and find enlightenment.
For her journey will last a life time, and her thirst will never end.

When woman closes her eyes, and looks upon her heart, does she feel the wings of spirit lifting her closer to the heavens?
Maybe drawing her closer to home, with each breath she takes. Do you remember the way home, when you close your eyes and look upon your heart?

When woman ends her day and lays her head down, she will rest in the arms of the Great Spirit.
Who will carry her to worlds where she will dance upon stars and write poems with an angel wing quill.
She will meet with the Masters of the Universe they will greet her as their sister and drink tea made from rainbows.
And when the dawn comes she will awaken with these treasures written on her soul.

Woman and Wind are one
Wind and Voice are one.
Woman and Fire are one
Fire and Dance are one.
Woman and Water are one
Water and Birth are one.
Woman and Earth are one
Earth and Life are one.
Woman is the voice that dances with the glorious birth of all life. For the Divine Spirit is in all things as the wind blows and the fire burns and water gives life, woman says her prayers to heal our Earth.

Woman can hear the hunger and pain of those who hide in the darkness of fear.
She is the healer who will dance the prayers that feed the hunger and sing the song that heals their pain.
She is the Shaman who soars like the eagle and brings light to their darkness as she leads them to their higher truth.

Woman is a majestic spirit of life, with creative forces flowing through her thoughts of the universe and her oneness with it all.
Woman rises above all doubt as she stands with love in the breathing heart of her God.

Woman is like the wolf that stands on the edge of the forest listening and feeling, guided by her intuition.
She instinctively follows her soul voice, her God voice from within.
As she knows this voice never lies to her.
Just as the wolf knows the forest will never lie to her.

Woman is spirit in the wind, she is the playfulness in the leaves as they dance across the ground.
She will hear the joy and laughter of the birds in the sky above the chattering shadows in her mind that say "you can't".
With sister wind in her face woman will only know "Yes I can because I am!"

Woman is the music in the song of Life.
She is the melody the angels sing as they greet the birth of all creatures great and small.
Woman is the call of the wild in nature.
She is the voice that dances across the land as she touches the heart of the wind.
Showing compassion and love to all creation.

Woman is the voice in the wind, the dance in the fire, the motion of the waters and the texture of the earth.
Woman sees the color of sound as her God speaks to all creation.
For she is the living message of Oneness and Love.

Woman chants her mantras to the dawn for the rising Sun calls her.
She will breathe in the Angel of the Sun to purify her thoughts, her breath, and her words.
Like the Arabian stallion that dances across the desert in freedom of Spirit.
Woman will dance this day in her freedom of Spirit and Life.

Woman knows her eternal life and feels the love of heaven now as all creation whispers their love for her.
She will touch the consciousness of oneness with her breath as her soul moves in rhythm with the universe around her.

Woman knows her search for the consciousness of God is an inside job.
She knows the relationship is between the music and the words as she sings her prayers and dances with Spirit. Woman stands in the universe with her thoughts of Oneness as she touches the heart of all life and embraces the consciousness she has found.

*Woman never speaks of charity she just does it.
She will not defend the truth she just walks it.
Woman writes diversity across the sky in many
colors, and knows One God with infinite names.
She walks hand in hand with all her sister as they
touch all creation through the loving creative
energy of Oneness.*

Woman opens the door to the mirror as she reaches through and touches the heart of her reflection.
She will embrace the truth and kiss the wisdom and knowledge of Self Realization.
She knows she has come from many worlds with many lives as she offers her healing prayer to all who will listen "within all life, lies the kingdom of peace and your time is now" is what she tells them.

Woman pays homage to the voice of her soul as she dances amongst the flowers and butterflies in her garden. She tastes the sweetness of her thoughts that draw from her oneness with joy as the light of creation surrounds her every step.

Woman rests at the center of her God's heart, she dreams of beautiful dances and sweet candy made of nectar.
She is the waking thought of the sunrise, the scent of morning dew.
All flowers want to grow up to be a woman.

Woman will paint the color of rainbows upon the ground she dances on, as she journeys through life with her song.
She will dress the flowers and the trees with delicious poems of kindness and compassion as she feeds the wild beasts and little creatures of the forest.
She will touch the heart of the Sun and kiss the Sky as her thoughts turn to a pool of love for all who cross her path.

Woman will ride upon Spirit as though she were music floating through the air.
She will rise into the consciousness of oneness like the colors of the coming dawn.
Her voice will echo of peace through the wind and she will be called by her angel name throughout the sisterhood of the world.
For she will lead the new world in a dance of oneness with Spirit.

Woman will travel through her mind hand in hand with her soul clearing out the wreckage of her past. She will cut the baggage of her thoughts from her heart that weight her down.
She is committed to a consciousness of love that will not harbor shadows of pain and hurt from the past. As she steps forward into a new day of life.

You will ride upon the holy spirits of your truth as you carry the message of life to all your sisters around the world. Speak of love, joy, and compassion to all whose path you cross woman. Feed the hungry who seek truth of their highest good and deepest beauty.
As woman will lead the path to the kingdom of heaven here on earth.

Let us turn our heads to the glorious sky of love and joy.
Raise your hands and welcome the rain from the heavens.
As you purify your thoughts and welcome the angels of love. Feel your love, listen to your soul, and dance with your spirit.
You are the woman who wears the colors of her heart.

The journey of a woman's path is led by her soul and guarded by the sacred dance of her Angels. Her story is written on the wind and heard throughout all creation.
Her love flows like a river of holy water quenching the thirst of beast and man as she paints her thoughts of life in a song with the colors of a woman's heart.

When woman is quiet she is touching the heart of silence, she is in the world of creation listening to the whispers of all life.
She can feel the breath of all creatures large and small as she moves so gentle through the air with her thoughts.
She is at peace with Spirit in both worlds, because both worlds know her by the colors of her heart.

Woman is the music in the sun rays that reflect the rainbows upon the skies.
She is the dance between the wind and the clouds that shapes the magical images that touch so many lives.
Her love is the bright light that shines from the stars of the universe.
Woman is the space between the notes of a great song that ties it all together with the colors of her heart.

Woman will touch the face of her God with the glorious joy she has for life. She will dance upon her thoughts of how the angels surround her every step.
Her path is one of love and kindness for the world she creates in her mind, as she writes her song of new beginnings and the rising dawn.
For on the face of her God, are the colors of her heart.

Woman writes the holy book of dancing angels.
She will paint the color of sound in the hearts of those around her.
Woman molds the texture of the earth in everything she touches.
She is the path of loving creative energy that whispers in the ears of the artist.
Her song in life is manifested through the colors of her heart.

Woman looks to the stars in heaven from which her spirit first ascended. She will listen to the voice of her true nature and remain undaunted by all others. She sees her true purpose is to build her bridge of light and love as many sisters and daughters will follow her journey into the Great Consciousness of Oneness.

Angel Woman

He will only see her as the angel in his dreams, as she holds the kiss that answers his cries to God to be loved.
Woman will teach him the rhythm in the song of love as an angel would show a lost man the way home.
She will fill his thirst to be loved as though she were the rain falling from the heavens.

Listen to the gentle songs of your angels as they come to heal your hurt and pain.
See them carry you to the breathing heart of your God, as you rest in this consciousness of love that surrounds you.
Let the colors in the light wash away your doubts, and fill your thoughts with love and kindness.
Then send this healing energy to others in need.

Woman hears the wind speak, as the Angels sing to her.
She dances with life as she is touched by the great compassion.
She speaks through her soul of the Consciousness of Oneness because she is a true healer to all and she serves with love. This human angel of the light.

Woman blends her worlds of heaven and earth as she walks her path of Self Realization.
She can feel the texture of the stars as easily as she will hold a palm full of water from the well in the earth.
She will walk with the whispers of her God echoing in her every thought, for she is a human angel amongst all the angels.

Woman is like the Angel of Joy as she holds hands with life and dances to the colors of her heart.
Woman will rise above adversity as though it were a board game she has mastered and can't be beat!
She will greet each step she takes as though it were a new friend bringing laughter and pleasure to her every thought of new beginnings.
Woman is the human Angel of life creating songs of love and laughter to share with those around her.

Woman will be like the Angel of the wind. Her dance will rise above or journey beneath, she will move around or go through what ever obstacles stand before her. The echo of her breath is felt around the world by all creation as she dances an unstoppable force in her certainty. Many a magus has called upon her to turn the windmill of their mind.

*In quiet contemplation she reviews her life.
Knowing that she has followed her endeavors, the desires of her soul, she has moved through her life in full spirit.
She has held hands with the Sun and the Wind and danced in the glory of all life.
Woman has heard the voice of All Creation and embraced the calling, this woman we call the Angel of Love.*

There is not a more beautiful Angel then you.
Born in the creative energy of the Consciousness of Oneness.
You reside in the breathing heart of Love.
Your dance with life is the reflection of joy and happiness that helps to heal our world.

Created by the great Consciousness of Oneness in all their glory and beauty are the angels of the heavens and the earth. Designed by an all loving energy of light they walk with us through life ever present and joyful.
These angels of the light within us and around us are the reflection of who we really are, as well as the gift we embrace one another with.

Consumed by the source of light she meditates on the beauty of her world.
Love and kindness is her work, with this energy she heals many lives.
On a timeless path between the heavens and the earth this human angel sends the message of inner peace and love as she walks along the shores touching all hearts.

Dance with me in the light of your path.
Hold my hand as we step through the darkness.
Listen to my whispers in your ear of love and kindness.
For I have heard the voice of your heart and we are one.

The angel comes to her because her thoughts manifested him.
Her love so real, so powerful so beautiful.
Their oneness so real, their consciousness so vibrant.
They embrace the creation of their love as they were created to do.

In her silence she hears the wind speak, the other Angels, they sing to her as she dances with life. Touched by the great compassion she is a true healer to all. Her soul talks of the Consciousness of Oneness because she serves with love, this human angel of the light.

Let us hold the light we our and invoke our highest love.
We will close our eyes and raise our thoughts to the heavens.
Touching all life with this light we heal many lives.
You are an Angel of Light here and now, see nothing less!

Let us touch the consciousness of love from which we come. We are our most creative thought, the art of our life, and the great manifestation of our Soul. Let us bend our thoughts around this idea of expressing our love to the highest good in which we are.

The Laws by which woman will live and who she is are written across her eyes, across her heart and recorded in her soul by the Divine Feminine Consciousness of her God.
Woman writes her book with the quill from an angel's wing, she writes her journey, and is the only one who can sing her song.
This is the book of laws she signs and gives to her daughters to read as they are born into the oneness of Divine Feminine Energy.

Moon Woman

Like the butterfly released from its cocoon, Moon Woman has done the work to free herself from the chattering shadows that danced in her mind.
No longer is she bound to the lies that restricted her transformation, as she has stepped through the veil of fear and into the light of her Supreme Self.
She has AWAKENED to the true beauty of her life.

Moon Woman bows her head to her heart, she knows the source of her being.
She embraces all possibilities of her desires and then releases them to an all giving universe of love.
She is clear about her journey as her course is set for her highest good.
Her message is clear, "I am and always have been the breathing heart of my God."

Moon Woman does her sacred dance upon the water.
Guided by the rhythm of her heart, led by her soul, empowered by the elements she moves freely like the smoke lifting from the fire.
The dance is for all her sisters to heal.
Spirit answers the calling of Moon Woman.

Moon Woman does not defend her intuition, she embraces it.
She does not defend her truth she lives it.
Guided by the inner voice of her soul, she is at peace in her world.
She welcomes all her creativity to manifest in the beauty of life.
Her path is one with the Universe of abundant love and truth.

Moon Woman gazes into her soul as she listens to the voice of all that has been and all that is to come. Above all else she understands the presence of this voice as a guide that has held her hand through all her lives.
She knows this voice as the eternity of her journey. Never a betrayal, never an abandonment, never a lie, this voice has been.
She leans her will into the wisdom of her soul, the voice from deep within her gut.
This is the voice from which her God speaks to her.

Moon Woman is like the volcano, her power comes from deep within her.
It is not held nor grasped from the outside. She knows her inner fire burns deep.
Like a child coming from its mother's womb, Moon Woman will rise from deep within her sisters, to help the people of the earth in their healings and their sufferings.

Moon Woman touches the heart of all life, from the creatures of sea to the giants that walk the earth. She communes with them, she journeys with them all.
Moon Woman follows the voice of her soul and heals all with the love of truth.
That our journey is one that our consciousness is one, all who touch their heart have felt these words that heal our world.

Touched by her highest calling Moon Woman listens to the whispering wind around her. In solitude she prepares for her journey knowing she will walk away from what was, and into the "what is" of life. Trusting her inner voice, she follows the source of her being. Moon Woman leads the path for many women to follow to their new beginnings.

Moon Woman bares herself to the world unafraid, she does not hide who she is nor will she be stopped as she climbs to the top of the mountain to touch the night.
Moon Woman communes with all life, unwilling to separate the weak from the strong she see all things equal before her God.
Moon Woman holds hands with the sky that carries her song of Oneness around the world for all to hear.

As the pages fall from the old book, Moon Woman walks toward the light.
Letting go of what she was told to be and how to think she enters new beginnings with a different mindset for her life. Her learning no longer dictated by male law, all her knowledge and wisdom will come straight from the Source of all life.
Empowered by the Light she writes a different book now and gives that to her daughters of the world.

Moon Woman is the reflection of the music in the night.
She is the beauty of her soul as she sings her prayers and poems of her relationship with the universe.
She has washed her mind and quenched her thirst in the river of her God.
She has baptized her sister with love and dried her off with the wing of an angel.
Moon Woman walks in between the worlds dancing with the spirits of joy, laughter, kindness and compassion as she holds hands with those who awaken to their highest truth of self.
She dances inside the woman who embraces the colors of her heart.

Woman will quiet her mind as she breathes the night air.
She will touch the music of the stars with her thoughts.
And she will dance around the moon with the spirits of the night.
Her soul is one with the universe, her heart is one with heaven.

Butterfly Woman

A Butterfly Woman will dance upon the flower of life in full beauty of her soul.
She will dress in the consciousness of oneness and sing about the angels of the sky, and the angels of the earth, as they will sing back to her.
She will touch the heart of many peoples garden and bring beauty and love as she will teach others to dance upon their flower of life with her song.

The colors of a woman's heart are reflected on the wings of a butterfly, just as her thoughts of life are reflected in the songs of the angels.
Her compassion for creation is reflected in the dance of a ballerina, as her soul is reflected in the brightness of the rising sun.
Woman touches the heart of her joy with the awakened thoughts of herself and journey.

Woman goes to the forest of her mind and frees her thoughts as though they were butterflies once trapped in her head like hostages to a certain way of thinking.
Her thoughts now become like beautiful creatures of the sky, lightly touching down upon the flowers of love and abundance and freedom to be herself.

Woman sees the beauty of the butterfly through the reflection of her Self.
Her cycle is not so different from her sister butterfly in her transformation to her highest Self Beauty. She dances in the brilliants of her creation, and as they touch the colors of their lives, their message is the same we offer great love and beauty to all who seek to see it.
"She is the Butterfly Woman."

Butterfly Child knows all love, she flies in the moon light with the angel of earth.
She speaks only the language of the heart, to all who cross her path.
In her thoughts she paints her music in color, and sings to the heavens.
She is the poem in the heart of the gentle whispers of your soul.

Gentle is the flight of her dance with life.
Softly she loves, as she touches your thoughts.
Like rainbows dancing in the sky,
With the colors of love, kindness and compassion
Butterfly Woman brightens the world with her song.

Softly the butterfly whispers:
Our magic is in our flight, beauty is in our touch.
We can unfold the freedom of your heart.
Sing with us about our Oneness with the Universe.
Fly with us, you are such beautiful creatures.
You Human Beings.

Without the humbly crawl and the creative thoughts of the caterpillar, Butterfly Woman would not complete her transformation and be able to kiss the flowers or dance with the sky as she beholds her true beauty before all creation.

Butterfly Woman touches the heart of her world, as she embraces it with absolute love.
She dances upon her thoughts of life with a lovely song.
Butterfly Woman kisses these words that come from her lips as though she were drinking spirit from the Holy Grail itself.
Her spirituality flows through the fields of her dreams like rain drops falling from the sky.

Freed from the bondage of her cocoon, she emerges in brilliant colors of life.
Rising in all her beauty, on a journey guided by her soul, with her course set to experience love in all its glory, she embraces her creation.
She is the Butterfly Woman.

The Dance of Butterfly Woman is the story of her journey.
As she came from crawling into darkness to her freedom of flight into the light.
Butterfly Woman speaks to all women as their independence unfolds in mind, body, and spirit.
Beautiful is the woman as she dances in full color.

Butterfly Woman will touch the sky with all her love.
She will stand bare foot upon her Mother Earth as she holds hands with the angels of the Sun and they will dance in the wind their sacred dance of womanhood.
She will sing her song of healing for the oneness of all life.

A butterfly never sees a weed it only see a beautiful life force from which it will seek to sip nectar from. Like the Butterfly Woman she will see beauty in all life she will seek to share that life force with all she comes in contact with.
Because it is in her nature to see this beauty and not the prejudices in others.

A Butterfly Woman will expand in the beauty of her heart as if she is floating in the hand of her God.
She will hear the music in her heart as though it were chimes playing her melody of love.
She will dance upon beautiful images of flowers in her mind and sip the nectar of joy throughout her day.
Butterfly Woman will bask in the sun light of her highest thoughts and see herself as a creative loving energy of life.

Woman is a Divine Soul experiencing life's journey. Like the butterfly that touches flowers sipping nectar with joy and pleasure. She dances across the sky embracing each moment in the sun light as she glitters with laughter of love for her life.

The Gospel of Woman

In the heart of the fire, woman dances within the flames of life.
She will wash her hands in star dust before placing them upon the wounds of her sister.
She will wear the kingdom of heaven upon her feet as she leads the path for all children to follow.
Her eyes will embrace all creation with the kiss of life.

Sense the beginning of human beings, woman has counseled with the Sages, dined with the Masters and taught with the Prophets.
Woman birthed the Sages, breast fed the Master and raised the Prophets.
She has always been the blanket of the leaders man chose to follow.
Her voice gives song to the ideas others teach.
She will see herself as nothing less than the breathing heart of her God as she walks in the light of her mortal life.

Woman was created by the song of God and birthed through the womb of her Mother Earth.
Laid upon her mother's breast she is shielded by the wings of the Angels, as she is fed by the elements that surround her.
She will bring a love into the world to heal all life. And man will come to lie beside her, to be touched by the heart of this love.

Weaved throughout the fabric of the universe is the creative loving energy of the human angel called woman.
Created by the Great Consciousness of love this angelic life force teaches compassion and kindness to all earthly beings ready to learn the path of peace and love.

Lovers

He will hold her as though he was going to baptize her in the river of their love.
Naked are their emotions, vulnerable is the trust, how strong a love they have together as they bathe in oneness.
Let him softly bathe her with his Spirit, and she will lay in his arms as though she was being held by an Angel.

Let him kiss on her skin as though he was reading poetry to her.
Let his fingers move across her as if he were reading Holy Scripture in Braille.
He will press his heart against hers believing she holds his last breath.
And she will embrace his love, as though she had wings tilted against the wind raising her higher and higher.
These lovers of a timeless kiss.

Hypnotized by the scent of his woman as she caresses his face.
He dreams only of his love for her, for she is his Goddess.
He can only hear the beat of her heart as he breathes.
This perfect order of love he feels as she holds him.

Let his love for her dance in the colors of her feelings and emotions.
Let his lips taste the spirit of her consciousness as they merge into the oneness of being.
Let him embrace her as though their love will rise to the heavens and their spirits dance before the Gods.
Then he will have loved her as God made her to be loved.

*Let them stand amongst the clouds gently
embracing one another.
He will touch his heart as she kisses him softly,
floating through his thoughts.
She will feel his gentle love for her as he holds her.
Let them dance in the sky before God, with the
angels lifting them higher as they dance.
Their Spirits merge as they touch each other's
breath.*

Like a pool of water, Love will seek its own level, and as our spirits merge the vibration of love will fill our body, and our thirst will be quenched in the beauty of the moment.

There will be no separation between the spiritual and the temporal world for them.
Just as there will be no separation in consciousness or breath as they merge to their clearest thoughts of love.
As their bodies touch they will anoint each other with the sweet oil of oneness, and rise like a song to the heavens.

*To tell me to stop is to take my air away that my
lungs collapse, my lips turn blue and I die.
Yes my darling, but of course I will stop.
That I may transform into my thoughts and become
an ocean of love for you, instead of just a man.*

Was it the life before this one?
Or was it the life before all life,
that they loved so trustingly?
No form can separate this love.

*Woman will whisper new laws of romance to him.
Her words will be like rain falling on the parched
desert floor filling his mind.
Her touch will bind his will, and he will be like the
adept student.
As these lovers write their own book of love.*

Woman will not stand in the shadows of who she is and what she knows.
She will teach the wild beast to dance to her song and she will tame the storm within him.
Her knowledge of love will make him thirst for the rain.
As she will rein this love affair with the colors of her heart.

Woman is the voice of the wind that the beast in the forest stops to listen to.
She is the sixth sense that speaks to the creatures that walk our earth, the fragrance that rises from the wild rose on a hot summer day.
She is the song all men dream to sing, in hopes to kiss the words and taste her magic on their lips.

Created by the Gods to be adored with an untamable spirit woman holds majestic powers with her thoughts.
She will touch the sky with her breath and shift the stars with her eyes.
She will create texture in color with her beautiful song, and all life will love her.
Man will seek to touch the essences of what the Gods created.

He can only hear her thoughts of love as he holds her.
He can only see the light of her beauty as she dances in the meadow of his mind.
His desire to be with her is in the magic of the mantra she whispers "Oneness of Love."

He will labor to build their altar, she will sing a prayer of magic.
He will petition his God to give him the knowledge of love, she will summon the elements of passion.
He will sacrifice all other desires just to hold her with his kiss.
She will release all thoughts as she holds the magic of his passion against her body.

He will listen to her poems on lovers and learn to be the adept student of her teachings.
He will touch the library of her thoughts for she is the poet and he is the words.
Her knowledge of love and words will bring tears of joy to the stars in the night and make the moon scream in ecstasy. As woman will write their dance upon page after page and her book will be sung by lovers around the world.

She will breathe the magic of the night upon his thoughts and play soft music on his skin with her fingers.
He will hear the melody of her love as he craves to touch the colors he sees when he closes his eyes.
She will whisper poems of the moon as he steps into her world and gentle lifts her with his love.
She will welcome his love like the night welcomes the stars.

She will tell him of a love so ancient that it could only be told by God.
He will listen as if he were a blind man standing on the edge of a cliff hanging onto her every word.
She will lead him through this love as though she were the music and he were the notes to her song.
And they will touch a love so ancient and pure
It will glorify lovers around the world.
These lovers of a lost dance.

Dancing with Life

Woman stood in the park with naked feet feeling the fresh cut grass touching her life.
In thought she looked to the sky as if she were the sky and felt the rays of the Sun embrace her with warmth and love.
As she turned her head downward she could see the mystery of her oneness with her world.
Woman looked into the eyes of her shadow and said "I am not in love, I am love"!
And the shadow raised its arms over head with elbows bent, and hands tilted down in the shape of a heart.
Woman said to her shadow "I am not ridged in thought but flexible like the willow"
And the shadow stretched arms upward and bent like a rainbow.
Woman said to her shadow "I do not move so shyly when I enter the world of life"
And the shadow stepped back twice and spun around 3 times then leaped forward.
Woman said to her shadow "I am not a dormant mind, I am a creative expansion filled with the energy of light"!
And the shadow with bent knees and hands turning stretched arms outward then slowly rose up with head tilted back.
Woman said to her shadow "my heart is filled with abundant song and freedom from the bondage of lies of how I should be."

And the shadow with arms stretched out ran across the ground to the top of a tree shadow as though it were an eagle perched on a cliff ready to take flight through the sky.

Woman looked into the eyes of her shadow and said "my life is now and I will live it as if I were a prism casting colors of light around the world."

And the shadow lowered arms with head bowed, curtsied as the sound of church bells rang nine times.

A gentlemen walking by looked at the woman and said "woman why are you dancing with your shadow"? And she looked the gentleman in the eyes and said "I am not dancing with my shadow kind sir …. I'm dancing with life."

Woman and Horse

Woman hears the soft spoken words of this creature called horse telling her "Come, come and dance with me."
Let us touch the hearts of the unspoken words between us.
Let us hear the thoughts we share in the oneness of our lives.
Woman watches the slow movement of the gentle giant that speaks to her, it is the language of their hearts.
She leans into the power of his dance that reaches out to her in this majestic relationship.
Attuned to the heavens and the earth, she will ride before the Gods on a creature called horse, as was done in a time when the soul voice ruled the world.
A time when all creation could feel the thoughts of one another as they touched the silence.
The gentle movement whispered "Come, come and dance with me"
Together they will run with the wind, beneath in the Sun.
They will dance before the Gods and the Gods will be pleased as they see the old way return.
And the soul voice speaks through the language of their hearts. "Come, come and dance with me."

Woman and the Angels

How beautiful the woman looks as she stands in her garden of life with the sun rays cascading down upon her.

Woman shall write her prayers upon the wings of Angel of the Sun, as the Angel will carry them to the most high.

She will call upon the Angel of the Sun to shine light on the fields and light the path for those who have wandered into darkness.

She will call upon the Angel of the Waters to quench the thirst of the fields that man as plowed and planted, and bless the crops to feed the multitudes.

For her thoughts are Holy and lay upon the altar of the earth as she walks through the fields each step a pray.

Woman will sing a beautiful song of glory as the Angels dance and bring sunshine and rain to her Mother Earth.

Her breath is one with the Angel of the Air as her words are carried in the wind, and all will hear the whispers of woman as she speak of peace, kindness and compassion.

The Angel of the Air will carry her message to the most high in the kingdom of her heaven, and touch the heart of all life that is created on Mother Earth.

As each breath that woman takes she knows it comes from the breathing heart of her God.

Woman will stand in her garden of life with the Angels of the heavens and the earth as her thoughts are Holy and send a thousand blessing to those on their journey into eternity.

To Dance Upon a Rainbow

Woman sat at her desk looking out the window, as she smelled the air from the fresh fallen rain. Thinking to herself how her journey across the bridge has taken her to midway, she smiles for she knows all life is in perfect order around her. Gazing at the park she sees a small child running, laughing with joy at the freedom she knows and the freedom woman remembers only so well.

Woman watches the young child curtsey to a rose bush and dance around it as though it were her partner in a favorite song. Child sings to the sky as though she is a Rock Star and the park is full of people who have come to hear her beautiful voice, and woman remembers the song only too well.

Child runs through the park on fresh green grass as though she were a wild mustang galloping across the meadow feeling the wind on her face. Free, free, free the child feels as the woman touches her thoughts of an undaunted life so young.

Woman sits at her desk looking out the window as she watches the little girl climb into a swing and start to sway back and forth. Higher and higher she will go remembers the woman.

As the little girl swings she feels the rush of excitement in the moment, and in the moment the child looks across the park and into a window, were eye to eye woman meets child with smiles of love and oneness for the flight of the swing.

Child smiles as she sees the old woman standing behind the woman at the desk

For the old woman remembers so many times she sat at her desk with window open watching the rain fall and watching the park grow in beauty. She smiles back at the little girl and the child smiles back as the woman sits at her desk listening to the laughter that echoes from the park.

Looking to the sky child see the rainbow, and as if in a dream she reaches to touch the colors and hold them in her hand, and as her hand stretches out the woman too stretches hers out.

The old woman knows the dance only to well as she pulls the two hands together and ascends into the sky. The blue birds follow the flight of the three as far as they can, yet they go so much higher as they reach the bend of the rainbow, all holding hands dancing in a circle upon the rainbows bend in laughter and song. Together they are one so intertwined in life. They sing of love and joy with bellies full of warm and soothing memories. They drink tea made of rainbow nectar to quench their thirst of dreams they share.

The sun rays kiss the child on her face as she swings back and forth dancing upon the rainbow in her thoughts.

And the old woman smiles as she watches the woman at her desk looking out the window at the fresh fallen rain as the child plays in the park of dreams.

The Child at the Pond.

Woman once sat under a tree near a pond to meditate, and sat there holding three small rocks in one hand, and three rose petals in the other hand, with palms, up eyes closed and opened heart. As she cleared her mind an image of her heavenly Father and all his sons with the Holy Spirit appeared. Then she saw the heavenly Mother and all her daughters with the Holy Spirit appear. Watching as they merged into one great consciousness, the rocks rolled out one hand, and the petals blew away in the wind out of the other hand. She wept in joy, as she was now looking at her God.

As she leaned over the pond to wash the tears from her face there was the most brilliant and beautiful reflection she had ever seen. As though it was a seamless garment of love and light, she couldn't look away. It seemed to her the reflection was pointing to the other side of the pond. Bewildered she looked, and saw a young child looking at her covered in white light, smiling so happy, so beautiful, the child was waving. She wanted to go to the child, for she knew the child, she loved her, their eyes looked into each other's, and saw infinite life time's spent as one soul. She was compelled to go the child. She had to touch the light. Suddenly she felt the reflection in the water touch her hand and in looking down the reflection had vanished, she looked back across the pond and the child was gone too. She dropped her head in sorrow; gone, gone, gone was it all.

She decide to leave that spot and find another and as she walked across the grass in bare feet it felt as if each blade of grass was speaking to her, telling her of the cycle of life. She stopped and closed her eyes to listen and felt a light breeze dry the tears from her face and kiss her. In that instance she felt every particle of her body start to expand and separate into infinite particles but there was no pain and they merged into everything around her, and she heard everything speaking of their many lives in their cycle of life and she understood it all. Everything they said made sense, she could feel the presence of it all and was at peace with all that has happened and all that was to come.

Somehow she was able to take a deep breath in union with what she had become and release it. When she opened her eyes again she was still under the tree by the pond. Holding three small rocks in one hand and three rose petals in the other, she got up and tossed them into the pond. She watched the ripples as they expanded across the water. Then she turned to walk away, and as she was leaving, it as though mysteriously echoing, she could hear the soft giggle of a child.

Her Song

Woman stood upon the shores as she listened to the ocean song.
She watched the waves as they rolled up to her feet tugging gently for her to come join them.
As the moon glistened down on the water, Woman raised her hands to the night and shouted……
"I am Creation"
It was as if the stars above shifted at the echo of her words.
She looked down at her feet where an empty conch shell laid.
As if it were an angel's trumpet, Woman blew through the shell into the night crossing the ocean.
Off in the mist whales replied aloud, turning their course to greet her song. Woman ran along the edge of the beach chased by the hand of the sea as it tickled at her feet.
Freed from all inhibitions she shouts to the nights air "Bring me wind!"
A soft gentle breeze blows against her as if it were the fingers of God combing her hair back out of her face.
Dancing across the sand as though she were in flight, Woman leaps into the air as if to fly amongst the angels.
She stops and listens, she can hear the dolphins and calls to them as if they were her brothers and sisters. The dolphins tell her ancient poems of the world she lives in and the worlds to come.

Woman answers the creatures of the sea through the sound of her conch shell. The sound she sends is as ancient as the poems she listens to.
Woman stands in the moon light with her hair in the wind and bare feet touching the love of the sea. As if the whole world was listening Woman shouts into the night,
"I give birth to the Joy of my world through the breath of my song for I am one with all life"!
As a voice in the night whispered back to her; you are the birth of my magic and your path is the story of all my creations.
Woman reaches out into the night as if she is touching the heart of the voice that whispers.
She softly sings her song to the wind as the oneness of the night is in rhythm with all that surrounds her.